BRAZIL ABCs

A Book About the People and Places of Brazil

by David Seidman

illustrated by Jeffrey Thompson

Special thanks to our advisers for their expertise:

Patricia Sobral, Ph.D.
Brown University

Susan Kesselring, M.A., Literacy Educator
Rosemount–Apple Valley–Eagan (Minnesota) School District

PICTURE WINDOW BOOKS
Minneapolis, Minnesota

Editor: Jill Kalz
Designers: Joe Anderson and Abbey Fitzgerald
Page Production: Melissa Kes
Art Director: Nathan Gassman
Associate Managing Editor: Christianne Jones
The illustrations in this book were created digitally.

Picture Window Books
5115 Excelsior Boulevard
Suite 232
Minneapolis, MN 55416
877-845-8392
www.picturewindowbooks.com

Printed in the United States of America.

Library of Congress Cataloging-in-Publication Data
Seidman, David, 1958–
Brazil ABCs : a book about the people and places of Brazil / by David Seidman ;
illustrated by Jeffrey Thompson.
p. cm. — (Country ABCs)
Includes bibliographical references and index.
ISBN-13: 978-1-4048-2248-1 (library binding)
ISBN-10: 1-4048-2248-8 (library binding)
1. Brazil—Juvenile literature. 2. Alphabet books. I. Thompson, Jeffrey (Jeffrey Allen),
1970- . II. Title.
F2508.5.S45 2006
981—dc22   2006027229

Oi! (OYE!)

That's "Hi!" in Portuguese, the language of Brazil. Brazil is the largest country in South America. It's the fifth largest country in the world and just a little smaller than the United States. Often hot and rainy, Brazil has huge jungles and a seacoast that tourists love.

Venezuela

Guyana

Suriname

French Guiana

Colombia

BRAZIL

Peru

★ Brasília

Bolivia

Paraguay

Chile

Argentina

Uruguay

Atlantic Ocean

FAST FACT:
Brazil's population is about 175 million.

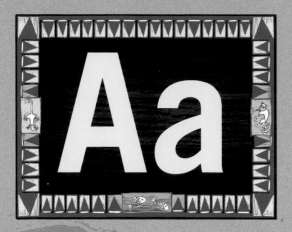

A is for art.

Brazil has all kinds of art, from pottery and paintings to the sculpture "Christ the Redeemer" overlooking the city of Rio de Janeiro. The stone statue is one of Brazil's most famous sights. Each of its arms measures 42 feet (12.7 meters) long—about as long as seven grown men lying head to toe.

FAST FACT:
Another famous Brazilian artwork is the São Bento church altar. Made of gold-covered wood, the altar stands more than 44 feet (13 m) tall.

Bb

B is for birds.

Brazil is home to some of the world's most colorful birds. Parakeets and parrots fill the Brazilian rain forests with their whistles and squawks. Toucans, woodpeckers, and hawks fly high among the treetops.

C is for Carnaval (kar-nah-VAHL).

One of Brazil's biggest festivals is called *Carnaval*. It takes place in February or March, in the days before Lent. During *Carnaval*, people wear costumes and masks. They go to parties and walk in parades. Rio de Janeiro's *Carnaval* celebrations are world famous.

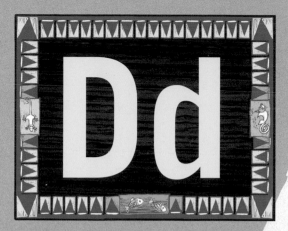

Dd

D is for dance.

Brazil is well known for dances such as the samba, the lambada, and the forró. These dances are graceful, fast, and filled with lively rhythms.

FAST FACT:
Samba is the traditional dance of *Carnaval*. Rio de Janeiro's best samba teams (called schools) compete in a grand *Carnaval* parade at the Sambódromo. One school may have thousands of members.

E is for economy.

Brazil's economy is busy and big. Most of the country's money comes from manufacturing, mining, and ranching. Despite the booming economy, however, many Brazilians are quite poor. The average wage for people working in Brazil's six biggest cities is just $332 per month.

FAST FACT:
Brazil produces the most tropical fruits in the world.

F is for flag.

The Brazilian flag is mostly green and yellow. In the center, it has 27 stars on a blue circle. Each star stands for one of the country's states (26), plus the capital city of Brasília (1). The phrase *Ordem e Progresso* means "Order and Progress."

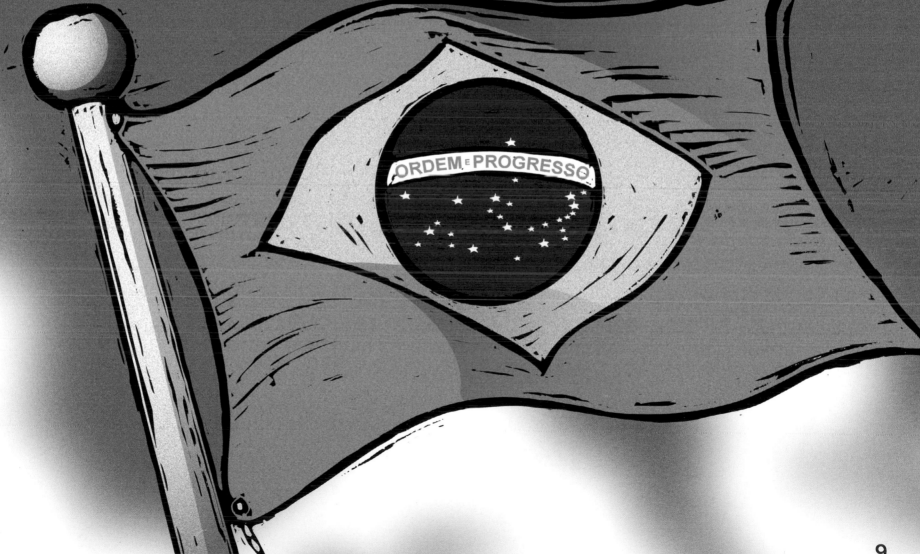

Gg

G is for guarana.

Guarana is a red berry that grows in northern Brazil. Brazilians use guarana in soda, chocolate bars, and even chewing gum. Some people say that guarana makes them stronger, healthier, and more energetic.

FAST FACT:
When the guarana fruit is ripe, it opens slightly so the seeds peek out. Then the berries look like eyeballs.

H is for "Hino Nacional Brasileiro."

"*Hino Nacional Brasileiro*" is the Brazilian national anthem. The song honors the Brazilian people. It also celebrates the country's strength and natural beauty.

National Anthem Chorus

Terra adorada! Entre outras mil
(O land we adore, amid a thousand others)
És tu, Brasil, Ó Pátria amada
(It is you, Brazil, the beloved land)
Dos filhos deste solo és mãe gentil
(You are the gentle mother of the children
of this soil)
Pátria amada, Brasil!
(Beloved homeland, Brazil!)

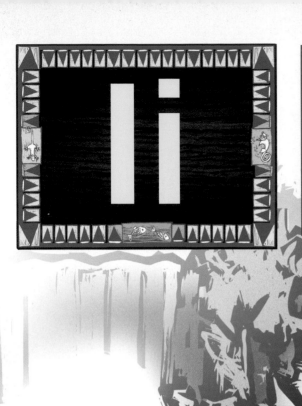

I is for Iguaçu Falls.

Iguaçu Falls lies on Brazil's border with Argentina and Paraguay. It is actually made of about 275 separate waterfalls. The falls stretch for 3 miles (4.8 kilometers) and attract more than 1 million visitors each year.

J is for jaguar.

Jaguars are big cats that prowl Brazil's rain forests. They can be up to 6 feet (1.8 m) long and weigh more than 300 pounds (135 kilograms). Jaguars are quickly disappearing from Brazil. Hunters often shoot them illegally. When farmers and homebuilders clear the land, they destroy the cats' habitat.

FAST FACT:
Jaguars feed on a wide variety of animals, including deer, turtles, and peccaries (wild pigs).

13

Kk

K is for kinkajou.

The wooly kinkajou lives high above the rain forest floor. It moves quickly and easily through the trees, grabbing branches with its tail. The kinkajou is a nocturnal animal, which means it is most active at night.

FAST FACT:
Kinkajous are sometimes called honeybears.

L is for language.

While most other Latin American countries use Spanish as their main language, Brazil uses Portuguese. The two languages are very similar. For example, "one, two, three" is "*uno, dos, tres*" in Spanish and "*um, dois, três*" in Portuguese.

15

Mm

M is for major cities.

Brazil has nearly a dozen major cities of more than 1 million people each. Many of these cities are shipping ports. São Paulo is Brazil's financial center, and, with more than 10 million people, it is one of the world's largest cities. Rio de Janeiro, with more than 6 million people, is about as big as the U.S. cities of Chicago and Los Angeles combined.

FAST FACT:
Most of Rio de Janeiro's poorest people live in slums, called *favelas* (fah-VILL-ahs), on the hills surrounding the city.

16

N is for names.

Brazilians can be wildly creative with their personal names and nicknames. Examples include Xerox, Welfare, Skylab, Dida, Zico, and Tostão. One family named their children by number, in French: Un (1), Deux (2), Trois (3) ... and well past Vingt (20)!

FAST FACT:
In Brazil, nicknames are often more widely used than given names. Brazil's president, Luiz Inácio Lula da Silva, is best known to Brazilians by his nickname: Lula.

O is for Ouro Preto.

Founded around 1700, the city of Ouro Preto ("Black Gold") was at the center of Brazil's gold rush. Beautifully designed houses, public buildings, and churches line the streets. In 1933, officials named Ouro Preto a national monument to preserve its many historic treasures.

Pp

P is for Pantanal.

The Pantanal is the world's largest wetlands area. Most of it lies in southwestern Brazil. It is roughly the size of the U.S. state of Iowa. The Pantanal's swamps, marshes, rivers, and lakes are home to more than 650 species of birds, 120 species of mammals, and 275 species of fish.

FAST FACT:
The world's largest parrot, the hyacinth macaw, lives in the Pantanal.

Qq

Q is for quindim (KEEN-ding).

A *quindim* is a Brazilian dessert made of sugar, eggs, butter or margarine, and coconut. A *quindim* usually comes as a custard or cake. The dish is so popular that it inspired a song, "*Os Quindims de Iaiá*," which means "Iaiá's *Quindims*." (Iaiá is a woman's name.)

FAST FACT:
Some people serve *quindim* with fruits or ice cream.

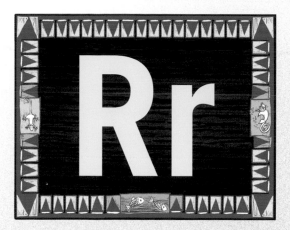

R is for rivers.

Brazil has more than 100 rivers, including some of the world's biggest. The São Francisco, which connects several Brazilian states, has been called the river of national unity, or togetherness. The Amazon River runs through Brazil's rain forests. It supplies the world's oceans with 20 percent of their fresh water.

Ss

S is for soccer.

The whole world plays soccer, but Brazilians are passionate about it. Millions play the sport. The Brazilian national team has won the World Cup championship more than any other team. Brazil is also home to Pelé. Many people believe that Pelé is the world's greatest soccer player.

FAST FACT:
In Brazil, soccer is called *futebol* (foo-chee-ball).

22

T is for timber.

Cutting and selling trees for timber is big business in Brazil, but it's hurting the world. The Amazon rain forest produces much of the world's oxygen and is home to many rare animals and plants. If the Amazon rain forest disappears, the whole world will suffer.

FAST FACT:
Rain forests get more than 80 inches (2 m) of rain every year.

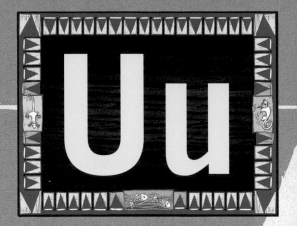

U is for universities.

Brazil spends more money on colleges and universities than most other South American countries do. Still, many Brazilians can't get an education beyond 12th grade. There aren't enough colleges and universities for all who want to go, and the schools accept only top students.

Vv

V is for vaqueiros (vah-KAY-rohs).

In northern Brazil, cowboys are called *vaqueiros*. In southern Brazil, they're called *gaúchos* (GOW-chohs). Cowboys run Brazil's cattle ranches. Famous for the cowhide clothing that protects them from the rough land, *vaqueiros* and *gaúchos* are said to be some of the toughest people in the country.

FAST FACT:
Brazil is the largest meat producer in the world. It has 165 million commercial cattle.

Ww

W is for wildlife.

The Pantanal, the Amazon rain forest, and other wild areas of Brazil are rich with wildlife. These regions are home to monkeys, alligators, turtles, otters, and snakes such as cobras and boa constrictors.

FAST FACT:
Wildlife travel is a popular type of tourism in Brazil. These trips allow tourists to view animals in the animals' natural habitat.

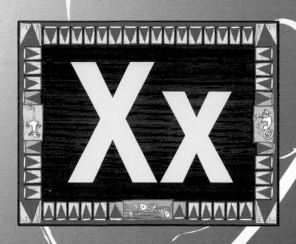

X is for Xangô (shan-GOO).

Although 75 percent of Brazilians are Roman Catholics, many other religions are practiced throughout the country, too. Xangô is the god of fire, thunder, and justice in one Afro-Brazilian religion. Xangô punishes evildoers with a double-headed ax.

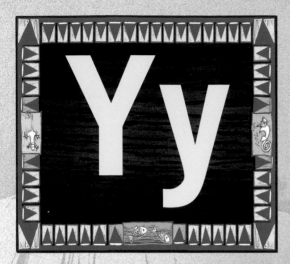

Yy

Y is for Yanomami.

In the forests of northern Brazil live 10,000 to 20,000 farmers and hunters called the Yanomami Indians. These people lived almost undisturbed by outsiders until the 1980s, when miners discovered gold on their land. After the miners killed many of the Yanomami for the gold, the government passed laws to keep outsiders from going into the area.

FAST FACT:
The Yanomami live in huge round huts that sleep dozens or even hundreds of people.

Z is for zabumba (zah-BOOM-bah).

A *zabumba* is a wide bass drum. It looks like a snare drum but has skin on both sides and produces a deeper sound. It often appears along with the triangle and accordian in small Brazilian bands to produce all kinds of dance music.

Brazil in Brief

Official name: Federative Republic of Brazil

Capital: Brasília

Official language: Portuguese

Population: about 175 million

People: 55 percent European origin; 38 percent mixed white and black; 6 percent black; 1 percent other (including Japanese, Arab, and Amerindian)

Religions: 75 percent Roman Catholic; 15 percent Protestant; 10 percent other (including Spiritualist, candomblé, and umbanda)

Education: Education is free. Students must attend school for eight years, from age 7 through 14. High school is available (but not mandatory) for students age 15 and older.

Major holidays: New Year's Day (January 1); *Carnaval* (February/March); Easter (March/April); Tiradentes Day (April 21); Labor Day (May 1); Corpus Christi (May/June); Independence Day (September 7); All Souls' Day (November 2); Proclamation of the Republic Day (November 15); Christmas Day (December 25)

Transportation: trains, cars, boats, airplanes

Climate: mostly tropical, but temperate in the south

Area: 3,404,786 square miles (8,511,965 square kilometers)

Highest point: Pico da Neblina Mountain, 9,888 feet (3,014 meters)

Lowest point: Atlantic Ocean, sea level

Type of government: federative republic

Head of government: president

Major industries: steel, aircraft, motor vehicles and parts, chemicals, textiles, shoes, cement, lumber, iron ore, tin

Natural resources: iron ore, manganese, bauxite, nickel, uranium, gemstones, petroleum, timber, aluminum

Major agricultural products: tropical fruits, beef, sugarcane, coffee, soybeans, wheat, rice, corn, cocoa

Chief exports: transportation equipment, iron ore, soybeans, footwear, coffee, cars

Money: real

Say It in PORTUGUESE

hi .... *oi* (OYE)

goodbye .... *tchau* (CHOW)

good evening .... *boa noite* (BOH-ah NOY-tay)

please .... *por favor* (POR fah-VOHR)

thank you .... *obrigado* (oh-bree-GAH-doo)

yes .... *sim* (SEENG)

no.. *não* (NAHNG)

Glossary

altar–a table used for religious purposes

Christ–Jesus Christ, the man whom Christians believe was the son of God

commercial–having to do with the selling of goods

economy–a country's trade in products, services, and money

habitat–the place and natural conditions in which a plant or animal lives

Lent–the 40 days during which Christians prepare for Easter

passionate–having very strong feelings

rain forest–a forest that receives more than 80 inches (2 meters) of rain during the year

Roman Catholics–people who believe in Roman Catholicism, a Christian religion; Christians believe that Jesus Christ was the son of God

timber–wood used for building things

To Learn More

At the Library

Gray, Shirley W. *Brazil*. Minneapolis: Compass Point Books, 2001.

Lichtenberg, André. *Brazil*. Austin, Tex.: Raintree Steck-Vaughn, 2000.

Weitzman, Elizabeth. *Brazil*. Minneapolis: Carolrhoda Books, 1998.

On the Web

FactHound offers a safe, fun way to find Web sites related to this book. All of the sites on FactHound have been researched by our staff.

1. Visit *www.facthound.com*
2. Type in this special code: 1404822488
3. Click on the FETCH IT button.

Your trusty FactHound will fetch the best sites for you!

Index

Amazon River, 21
animals, 13, 14, 19, 23, 25, 26
art, 4
birds, 5, 19
Brasília, 9, 30
Carnaval, 6, 7, 30
"Christ the Redeemer," 4
dance, 7
economy, 8
education, 24, 30
flag, 9
food, 10, 20
fruits, 8, 10, 20, 30
guarana, 10
Iguaçu Falls, 12
jaguars, 13

kinkajou, 14
language, 3, 15, 30
music, 29
names/nicknames, 17
national anthem, 11
Ouro Preto, 18
Pantanal, 19, 26
Pelé, 22
population, 3, 30
rain forests, 5, 13, 14, 21, 23, 26, 28
ranching, 8, 25
religion, 27, 30
Rio de Janeiro, 4, 6, 7, 16
São Paulo, 16
soccer, 22
Yanomami Indians, 28

Look for all of the books in the Country ABCs series:

Australia ABCs
Brazil ABCs
Canada ABCs
China ABCs
Costa Rica ABCs
Egypt ABCs
France ABCs
Germany ABCs
Guatemala ABCs
India ABCs

Israel ABCs
Italy ABCs
Japan ABCs
Kenya ABCs
Mexico ABCs
New Zealand ABCs
Russia ABCs
The United States ABCs
Venezuela ABCs
Vietnam ABCs